LITTLE BIOGRAPHIES OF BIG PEOPLE

HILLARY CLINTON

By Joan Stoltman

Gareth Stevens PUBLISHING

Please visit our website, www.garethstevens.com. For a free color catalog of all our high-quality books, call toll free 1-800-542-2595 or fax 1-877-542-2596.

Cataloging-in-Publication Data
Names: Stoltman, Joan.
Title: Hillary Clinton / Joan Stoltman.
Description: New York : Gareth Stevens Publishing, 2018. | Series: Little biographies of big people | Includes index.
Identifiers: ISBN 9781538209271 (pbk.) | ISBN 9781538212417 (library bound) | ISBN 9781538209288 (6 pack)
Subjects: LCSH: Clinton, Hillary Rodham–Juvenile literature. | United States. Department of State–Biography–Juvenile literature. | Presidents' spouses–United States–Biography–Juvenile literature. | Women cabinet officers–United States–Biography–Juvenile literature. | Cabinet officers–United States–Biography–Juvenile literature. | Women legislators–United States–Biography–Juvenile literature. | Legislators–United States–Biography–Juvenile literature. | Women presidential candidates–United States–Biography–Juvenile literature. | Presidential candidates–United States–Biography–Juvenile literature.
Classification: LCC E887.C55 S7585 2018 | DDC 327.730092–dc23

Published in 2018 by
Gareth Stevens Publishing
111 East 14th Street, Suite 349
New York, NY 10003

Designer: Samantha DeMartin
Editor: Joan Stoltman

Photo credits: series art Yulia Glam/Shutterstock.com; Cover, p. 1 Alexander Tamargo/WireImage/Getty Images; p. 5 VINCENT LAFORET/AFP/Getty Images; p. 7 Wellesley College/Sygma/Getty Images; p. 9 Boston Globe/Boston Globe/Getty Images; p. 11 Cynthia Johnson/Hulton Archive/Getty Images; p. 13 Brooks Kraft/Sygma/Getty Images; p. 15 Jeffery Markowitz/Sygma/Getty Images; p. 17 Spencer Platt/Hulton Archive/Getty Images; pp. 19, 21 JEWEL SAMAD/AFP/Getty Images.

Printed in the United States of America

CPSIA compliance information: Batch #CW18GS: For further information contact Gareth Stevens, New York, New York at 1-800-542-2595.

CONTENTS

Boldface words appear in the glossary.

Young Hillary

Hillary Diane Rodham was born in Chicago, Illinois, in 1947. Her dad owned a store that made window covers. Her mom took care of their home. She has two younger brothers, Hugh Jr. and Anthony.

Hillary's mother, Dorothy

Hillary always did really well in school and won **awards** for good grades. She was a Girl Scout and played several sports. She wanted to be an **astronaut**, but was told she couldn't be one because she was a woman.

On a trip with her church, Hillary heard Dr. Martin Luther King Jr. speak. He **inspired** her to help people. Hillary went to college in Massachusetts, then law school in Connecticut. There were only 27 women in her class at law school.

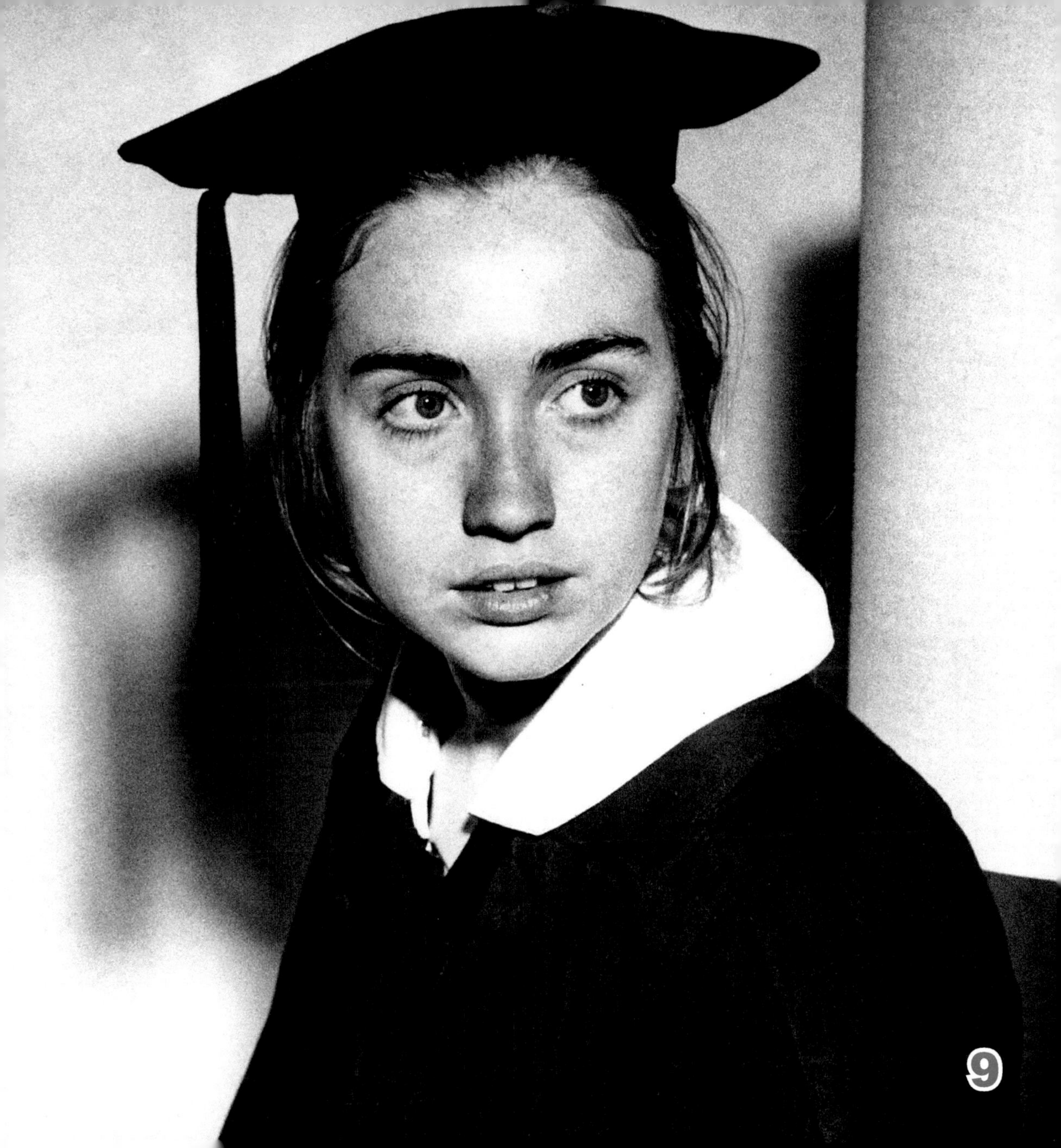

A Great Lawyer

As a **lawyer**, Hillary helped children with **disabilities**. She was voted one of the most powerful lawyers in the country by other lawyers—twice! Her husband, Bill Clinton, was the governor of Arkansas. That meant Hillary was the First Lady of Arkansas for 12 years! She helped children, the poor, women, and families.

Many Firsts

Bill Clinton was president of the United States for 8 years. Hillary had an office in the West Wing of the White House, where the president's office is. She's the only First Lady ever to do that! She's one of the most educated First Ladies ever.

As First Lady, Hillary worked hard every day for **civil rights**, women, and children. She visited about 80 countries, making important speeches that are still remembered today. Her work in health care stills helps over 8 million US children today!

Every Child Deserves A Healthy Start
Kids Speak Out For Health Care Reform

Hillary in Office

In 2001, Hillary became the first woman to be a senator for New York! She's also the only First Lady of the United States to ever be an elected **politician**. She ran for president in 2008, but wasn't chosen to be the **candidate** for her **party**.

UNITED STATES
SENATE

Hillary was President Barack Obama's secretary of state from 2009 to 2013. This is one of the most important jobs in the US government. She visited 112 countries and helped many people. She got many world leaders to talk to each other about working together for peace.

SEAL OF THE PRESIDENT OF THE UNITED STATES

In 2016, Hillary became the first female presidential candidate for a major party. She came close to winning! After she lost, she said, "Fighting for what's right is worth it." Many consider her the most important woman in the history of US government!

GLOSSARY

astronaut: a person who travels in a spacecraft into outer space

award: a prize given for doing something

candidate: a person who is trying to be elected

civil rights: the rights that every person should have regardless of his or her sex, race, or religion

disability: a condition that stops a person from being able to do certain things

inspire: to cause someone to want to do something

lawyer: someone whose job it is to help people with their questions and problems with the law

party: a group of people who agree about beliefs and ideas, and who work to have their members be a part of the government

politician: a person who runs for or holds a government position

FOR MORE INFORMATION

BOOKS

Corey, Shana. *Hillary Clinton: The Life of a Leader.* New York, NY: Random House, 2016.

Krull, Kathleen. *Hillary Rodham Clinton: Dreams Taking Flight.* New York, NY: Simon & Schuster Books for Young Readers, 2015.

Markel, Michelle. *Hillary Rodham Clinton: Some Girls Are Born to Lead.* New York, NY: Balzer + Bray, 2016.

WEBSITES

Meet Hillary Clinton
nick.com/mash-ups/videos/digital-short-kids-pick-the-president-hillary-clinton/
Watch this cool Nickelodeon video all about Hillary Clinton!

About Hillary
hillaryclinton.com/about/hillary/
This online scrapbook is filled with information, photos, and videos for you to check out.

United States Secretary of State
wiki.kidzsearch.com/wiki/United_States_Secretary_of_State
Read all about the job of secretary of state.

INDEX